ROMULUS BUCUR
MIRCEA CARTARESCU
Romania

DEDALUS

Poetry Network 4

Translations
from the Romanian of

ROMULUS BUCUR

&

MIRCEA CARTARESCU

First published in Ireland 1994
by The Dedalus Press
for
The Tyrone Guthrie Centre &
Poetry Ireland/Éigse Éireann

ISBN   1 873790 68 6

Design by   **Bordor**

The financial assistance of
The Arts Council/An Chomhairle Ealaíon,
and of the Arts Council of Northern Ireland,
is gratefully acknowledged.

This work is published with the assistance of the
Union pour la Valorisation du Patrimoine
(Association spécialisé du Groupe C.I.C —
Banque Scalbert Dupont)

The Dedalus Press
24 The Heath
Cypress Downs
Dublin 6W
Ireland

EUROPEAN POETRY TRANSLATION NETWORK

At the initiative of La Fondation Royaumont, France, a network of European centres dedicated to the translation of poetry by poets has been established. At present there are seven participating centres. They share a common dedication to establishing a body of contemporary poetry in translation, using also a common work-practice.

Two poets are invited to a host centre, where they will work for one week with a translator who produces the primary literal texts, and with a team of poets assembled for the occasion who, working as a team and in consultation with the visiting poets, are ultimately responsible for the final versions. These versions are subsequently published in the host country under a special imprint. Two poets from the host country are then invited to reciprocate this visit, to have their work translated and published in the same manner.

In this way, we aim to make available to readers of poetry throughout Europe a substantial body of the the finest contemporary poetry in all the languages of our common culture. It is a central feature of this initiative that the translations are ultimately the product of poet-to-poet encounters. By working in teams with the poets being translated we aim to break through to the original virtues of the poem, and carry as much of it as is possible over into the new language.

Future growth of the network will be organic, as we add new centres to the existing network.

In Ireland the project has the enthusiastic support of both Arts Council, in Dublin and Belfast, and the resulting books are published by the Dedalus Press under a special imprint.

EUROPEAN POETRY TRANSLATION NETWORK

Casa de Mateus
Portugal
La Fondation Royaumont
France
Reggio di Colorno
Italy
Institució de les Lletres Catalanes
Catalonia
P.M. Nomikos — The Idryma Thera Foundation
Greece
Chateau Pelês
Romania
Tyrone Guthrie Centre /Poetry Ireland
Ireland

Directors Ireland:

Bernard Loughlin   Tyrone Guthrie Centre,
Annaghmakerrig,
Newbliss,
County Monaghan.

Theo Dorgan   Poetry Ireland/Éigse Éireann
Dublin Castle,
Dublin 2.

ANNAGHMAKERRIG
NOVEMBER 1993

Romulus Bucur
Mircea Cartarescu
Romania

Translators:

Simion Dumitrache

Pat Boran
Heather Brett
Tony Curtis
Theo Dorgan

CONTENTS

Romulus Bucur

Mircea Cartarescu

ROMULUS BUCUR

Romulus Bucur was born in Arad, Romania, in 1956. A graduate of the University of Bucharest, he has been a member of the Writers' Union of Romania since 1990.

His poems, articles, essays and translations have been extensively published in the main Romanian literary magazines — *Romania Literara, Steaua, Orizont, Amfiteatru, Echinox, Contrapunct*, etc. His poems have been collected in *Cinci* (collective volume, 1982), *Greutatea Cernelii Pe Hirtie* (1984), and *Literatura, Viata* (1989).

katharsis

you use this term too often, *right honourable*
sometimes completely out of context
so, tell us
> what really goes on in that head of yours
you're just lucky that you live in a city
where nothing happens —
do you think *we* haven't read sadoveanu — *
but you know crime is on
the increase and you do come
from time to time to bucharest...

who do you think you are you're no match for us
one or a thousand like you, what does it matter
do you think we're going to waste our time, our money,
our men's energies
> you're wearing yourself out, you're stewing
> in your own juices
two or three days and you don't have a place to stay
except with an uncle from the National Salvation Front
who praises the miners or with another who's waiting
until the Socialist Labour Party and the *securitate* bring the
country
to order
so you have to walk and walk for hours
in the streets, trying to summon up pleasant
memories, or turn to a friend —
this one and that
we know all of them — and over a cup of tea
or coffee you swear at the government

or you queue in front of the embassy —
> they hand out visas like salami and eggs and
> everything else because you still get them

from us the way you got them before, so get this
into your head
  rat — because that's all you are,
  here or any other place
  you might think of going —
go to hell!

* Mihail Sadoveanu, author of, among other books, *The
Place Where Nothing Happens.*

the chrysanthemum spirit

the train gradually gaining speed
with every kilometre
breaking one by one your roots

    at the **dalles hall** autumn
    exhibition
    Ink's weight on paper
    had just been published
    what connection with chrysanthemums
    then a film with her

an almost formal visit
you gave her flowers too
(chrysanthemums naturally
though it was august)

she offered you jasmine
tea   she looked
hunted/haunted
under the word-shell
    around us omnivorous science
    proclaimed autumn

* * *

the void of an autumn day
greater than the leaf
that falls softly to fill it

(you search for your friends you
embrace each other you
still have trust)

nothing changes
another wooden layer
forms on
the peach stone

you bite greedily
and force a smile

nel mezzo del camin

then high nights would come
full of melancholy
endless

and you would remember unglorious homecomings
more those than the light
of small triumphs

cat lying in wait in a corner
your adolescent death

(still) young poet

"At fifteen I commenced
my studies with passion"

    Should the void between words
    be filled with music?
    night falls and you are
    more defenceless
    than a leaf

"At thirty I
rooted myself firmly
in the ground"

    it's spring   soul's
    a stray dog
    which barely broke
    its chain

glimpsed for one moment
disappearing forever after another
rows of signs
    on a palimpsest

En l'an trentième de mon age

Useful Work

Instead of writing
poems you'd be better doing
some Useful Work
mend something around
the house for instance

        certainly nobody
        dares
        come right out with it but
        you can see it in their eyes
        so from
        time to time
        I give the mugs some
        satisfaction

last sunday
I managed it
with a stuck lock
I took it to pieces
straightened something,
oiled it, searching

        for a tool
        I remembered
        my grandfather too
        had been a locksmith
        all his life he'd written
        poems   he'd chaired
        a workers' writing circle
        I took a wrench and a scrap
        of glasspaper
        forgetting myself
        I started
             to clean it

* * *

death comes on a windy day
the air is an electric epidermis
in cafés people sit in pairs
at tables

                suddenly the streets
are deserted & straight   a little girl
at play is being watched
by old maniacs under archways
frightened she disappears
a brown shadow falls

                you bend to pick up
a chestnut   you see a delirious crowd
prostrating at your feet
steam   bitterish the taste
                after a swig of tea

praise to the present moment

steam rising from the tea-cup
the contours of her body
guitar-notes spiralling up from the record
lines on paper starting to make sense

the gentleman in the pavilion of delight

say little
let the things speak —
a few clouds
the music blossoming
from every pore
cadence of drops
against the pane:

"vixen adept
in the game of cloud and rain"

song

and through my flesh passed
the wind-claws of hatred

my cry wards off
the demons   things
quake and
re-settle   I
am but a speck
of pollen caught in a whirlwind
my blood shaped
in the hands of a master craftsman
bursts out in thousands
of lotus flowers

        beauties of world and vanity
        things (I am told) I should deny
        cinders of lines, of songs, of little
                      pleasures
        to shine in the sunlight
        like a peeled wand
        to see nothing any more
        the wind to sing through me
        flowers floating downstream
        on the river

doc williams

*(fantasy portrait
            of a quasi-imaginary poet)*

the patients called him
to friends he was simply bill

CA(ro) DA(ta) VER(mibus)
he used to say
also speculating
upon the fact
that in german & english
death is masculine

and poetry in any language
is *violon d'encre*

14

easy to say destiny

the last night out from port
and the helm holding
towards home

record of a man's gestures — a few words
on a pharmacy label

and you catch desperately
at the hands of the clock

life — taste of a grape
crushed on the tongue

courage to

you should have the courage to remember
that last coffee you drank together
the rain which surprised you embracing
after the soppy film her departure
letters never sent from the army
in which you called her goddess and slut
poems in which homesickness
was stuffed in irony's tight shirt
you should have the courage to open wide
the windows of that castle of books
where you hide, and to look
at the wasteland you call your life
to set out from inside the walls of this town
and the next
                    and the next,
exhausted and famished in the umpteenth one
to sit on a bench
between a sleeping drunk
                    and a child at play

foundling

Sunday.
The family seated
around the table
"When I was your age . . ."
(The voices of the others
reach you
like the babble
of someone drowning
in the dregs of a huge bottle)

       "Your chance" —
       a friend leaving
       like a bus rounding
       a corner —
       "is that you still believe
       in the words we used
       to drug ourselves
       in our teenage years:
       love, friendship, honesty"

Autumn rings at your door
and leaves a foundling.

(katharsis)

I could copy the inscriptions
from any pair of headstones
you would have
to believe they were
my grandparents's   snow
covering them the cold and
emptiness of the graveyard
the fact that I too
could become
a block of ice
is sufficient transfiguration
for my tears
of those days
(now it seems
somehow out of place to cry)   even
if air sneaks
molecule by molecule
out of my lungs even
if seconds are
lead weights
dragging at my ankles

willow branch springs back
freeing itself of its burden
of snow

episode

1

what do you think you can salvage
from this shipwreck
in the poem's muddy waters
other than the image of a mare
thistles in her mane
staggering having met
the stallion

2

on the railway platform
among the cigarette butts
children, conscripts
hand in hand with girls
they met an hour ago
she's not home you are told
she's gone to the seaside
the idiot cassette repeating
sylvia's mother said ...

3

a handful of photos where
you appear in flattering poses
and out of this soul
with a coin in its mouth you can salvage
continuous and ever
more remote
departures

* * *

still light outside
you switch the light on inside
you look at the trees through the closed window
and the sky shoves you back in the armchair

                    (you should sweep up
                    the husks left
                    from this sunday)

you sense the void silently
spawning in every corner

the guitar man

you won't drive crowds wild
with it
and it isn't even
blue

(the empty beach
the empty cinema
the rubbish on the floor
the empty howl
in which you sit and sing
with terrible grief
of the world's life
written on sheets flayed
from living hearts
you sing of a woman
biting an apple
in front of a window
of good family fathers'
little sunday braveries
about yourself
  "jaded
    clownlike
       fanatical"
petering out like the footprints
of some wild thing in the open

viewed from space viewed from a distance
there seemed no limit to man's existence
viewed from a distance viewed from space
mankind seemed superfluous

in the little world of plasticine
when irony was still the queen)

the black car

This space with parks, benches
and quarreling lovers,
with its rain of darkness
dying slowly,
late passers-by
bloom and wilt, flowers
in the heavy air
        come on home, sky
        is a wet skin
        which small rats
        pull to cover the world
at your door a young wolf
with phosphorescent eyes
brings you fragile books
and again an error crosses your sky
and again the sun turns into lightning
and again there will be light

        you are an intellectual
        aren't you?

The night opens up, as do
two completely normal people
time for a little deflation
she says, and it seems
perfectly natural to you
        bats have eaten
           all the stars
              in the sky
      and fog   falls
      a lizard   sloughing
between   the graveyard
           and
the gas stations

all traffic lights
on red

Snow being carried outside town,
an idiot child
his family
aren't inclined to talk about

"Good, even like this" you say,
taking in a stride
the bus which has woken
all the dogs
in the neighbourhood.

a black car
creeping along
behind you.

insulin secretions

my girlfriend is venetian
her insulin secretions
help me find completion
for my soul

on the gondola of our love
with the zodiac above
I want to be the one who holds the pole

MIRCEA CARTARESCU

Mircea Cartarescu was born in Bucharest in 1956. He is at present Assistant Professor at the University of Bucharest.

He has published four collections of poetry to date: *Headlights, shopwindows, photogra*phs (1980), *Amour Poems* (1982), *Everything* (1985) and *The Levant* (1990).

He has also published prose, *The Dream* (1989) and an essay, *The Chymeric Dream* (1991). Two of his books have been translated into French, *Le Rêve* (1992), and Spanish, *El Sueño* (1992).

Mircea Cartarescu has twice won the Writers' Union Prize (1980, 1990) and the Academy Prize (1989).

To an Actress

Friend, sleep peacefully, your head on my pillow.
I'll sit and look at you.
We played a long time together.
The vodka bottle is half-empty and it's still
the middle of the night.
As for cigarettes — about two left.

What was *craic* between us and what was sexual,
clever conversation, films in the french library,
are all a finished season.
You will have other lovers.
I'll write other little verses.

Sleep peacefully on my pillow,
friend.
I wonder if your boyish chest,
like that of baudelaire's mulatto, will turn to me again.
I wonder how you'll be tomorrow at the station.
Do you know what the world is? You'll never know.
                                    I'll never know.
We'll roll your station down the cobbled platform,
keep in touch till summer comes.

You look weird without glasses.
Remember we saw this full moon from the 21.
That was the craic, making love all the time,
but everything is like a finished season.
You'll impress others with your style.
I'll write other little verses.

Wild Thing

what an animal! you stop at a watch-shop window.
your kind shouldn't be
let out. god, what tits,
through your Coca-Cola t-shirt, what nipples!
animal, beyond reach, in your blue jeans &
your silk panties. the raw meat you must be swallowing,
growling like a cat. O god,
what a woman!

not for us mere mortals. a man would die from
                              the cyanide of your hair
unless shielded in citroen metal, wadded with banknotes.
now you're looking at yourself in the window,
                              the ladies watches

sparkling on your face. would you prefer
the digital? that's your type. poorly-dressed men,
even two housepainters in their spattered clothes,
berets down to their eyes, are staring at you.

it's autumn on *Mosilor*, I'm tempted to compare
your bottom with the full moon. to you I'm nothing.
if I got the Nobel prize you'd be impressed by the money.
I'll never be on television
I'm no Arab prince.

what an animal. you move to the next window —
Hi-fi's at 11,000, 13,000 . . . you have beautiful
                              tarted-up lips
and clever eyes, imbecile eyes, what does it matter?
you live your scented, shampooed life in a daze
of clothes and hairy hands . . . you live beautifully,
                              you have sparkling teeth.

I hunch over the typewriter
reaping only disgust.
one of your breasts is worth my entire work,
as you pass through autumn on *Mosilor*
thinking probably of the Dunhill in your purse.

a fine day for the banana-fish

it's a fine day for the banana-fish.
I take the no. 90 as far as the university.
beloved reader, who would believe it's mid-december?
                 At *doamna ghica* the electric clock
(cum thermometer) shows +15°, and the pekinese
are without their little coloured waistcoats.
even the little branches on the trees seem greener and the
                        limestone of *ion minchu*
institute of architecture granulates in the sun.
sunrays everywhere. pinky-orange shop windows
                   crammed with slips, shirts, sweaters.
at *mirage* they even have deodorant and shaving cream
and in front of the cafe at *dunarea,* unbelieveable,
two stacks of crates, pepsi — they're selling it right
                             in the street.

what a day! what a fine day for the banana-fish!
a blue sky and women in piles of fox fur. I take
                      two bottles
of sparkling pepsi and sit
on a terrace varnished by sunshine
at a white iron table on a white iron chair.
squinting, I face the sun, my sheepskin left at home
and my plastic jacket starts to smell.
two cuties opposite drink pepsi too.
one's beautiful, blue eyes, and the kind of hair I love:
dark, with golden streaks, slightly wavy.
her coat open, her nice little breasts show
through a pretty coloured sweater.
beloved reader, in clear air the colours of the world are
                      so fluid
I'm afraid to breathe for fear of swallowing some
                   passer-by or skoda,
for fear the university would hurtle towards me.

the babes clear off, but I find another one to look at
and when all my pepsi's gone
I head for *cismigiu* into the chaos of the traffic
then from *kogalniceanu* take the trolley-bus back home.

beautiful morning for the banana-fish!

Motorcycle Parked under Stars

I'm a motorcycle parked under the stars, by the window of the
tv repair shop.
there's a draught from the archway. I'm pale, weak.
in the light left on in the shop a couple of cathode tubes,
pots of asparagus and cactus, wrought-iron shelves packed
with tv shells, AGFA cassettes and cables
glimmer, populating my loneliness.
for I feel lonely. galaxies swarm in my rear-view mirror,
stars steam in globular swarms, the radio sources send
                                        out their panting
all racing farther away, fleeing like murderers from
                                        the scene of the crime
leaving a trail of blood.

such silence. sometimes I wonder
what it would be to make love. because they speak of
                                        nothing else.
Every weekend they ride on me
and drag me out on the roads. I see hills, clouds, the sun
raindrops, trees tangled in the rainbow…
ah, my cylinders tick like mad. then I feel really alive.
they go into motels and make love.
they are the Masters, they feel free.
but how could anyone made of cells feel free?
…and then back to the archway, near some dusty *dacia*.

I'm thirsty for love. if only I could have that extension lead
and socket from the window,
I'd let my fingers glide on its white plastic skin,
                                        if it wanted
and if I had fingers. if I could live
even in the bio-electric field of the cactus…
soon, soon I will die, nothing achieved in this world,
                        they'll dump me on some scrapheap

they'll smash my headlight and my blown bulb will dangle
from two filaments of wire.
all my life I've helped others to make love
and I will die among coils, magnets and thistles.

I'm a motorcycle parked under the stars.
in the morning they'll ride out again, they'll grip
                              my handlebars, rev me up
and then out once more on the multi-coloured tarmac, among
russet hills, among blue mountains
through canyons threaded by rivers
over railway crossings, through pristine provincial towns
driving against the wind through raindrops and
                              exhaust fumes
eating up the kilometers.
could this be making love?
this is at least my consolation, *my* job, *my* love.
for this it's worth it to be lonely.

Do You Know the Country
where the Lemon Trees Blossom?

I'm waiting for tram 26 at the state circus.
the avenue is golden and the trees green, green and with
                                    so many leaves
that not even a renaissance painter could paint them all.
I stare after babes in blue jeans and baggy t-shirts
— across one's little tit is written JOGGING — I twist &
                                    turn around
a no. 5 passes and I put my finger to its red, warm metal
                                    and I think of a line
I even formulate it: 'this summer we have all become
mechanics, under clouds for hours'...

Mid-day, sunshine makes me dizzy, kids bring back
to their teachers rough branches of lilac
and lily-of-the-valley wrapped in cellophane
if you want to hurt your eyes look again
at the sun turn mauve, and on retina's deep night
inscribe faces and violet ribbons of bright light.
Glassy sun, hirsute moon,
this summer we have all become
mechanics, under clouds for hours
unscrewing the axles of the flowers.

at last, after a stream of 24's and 4's comes a 26.
I elbow through, climb on and find space at the back.
the sparkle of the avenue drives you crazy
but your heart is cold, because you have no love.
and you don't care for shop windows anymore and
all you can write these days are idiotic, useless letters.
I open *the utopian past* by himmelmann with its beautiful
                                    blue cover
and I read what goethe once of statues thought
bucharest, on the right and left, is and is not.

It was a Time of Flowers

in time you took on the status of a great power.
little by little you overran my avenues with your embassies,
your consulates, your agencies.
and today on the highway of my wishes
it was your blue eyes that came like two spotless limos,
their windscreens wolfing down the pink foliage of the
                                        cherry blossoms.

you have become a great foreign power.
from the zodiac your satellites take my picture in thousands of
poses, they spy on my insulin secretion.
they interrogate even my shaving kit
with menace they confuse my name with my surname,
                                        my age with my sex
the season with the trolley-bus, my thyroid with my star
while in a blizzard of pink floyd music I drink coffee
                                        obliviously.

nowadays I even address the driver as *effendi*
I even allow the shoeshine man to call me *boy*
I answer "yes, massa" to your lace collar
around one of your hairpins I tailor dresses out of dozens of
square metres of shop windows
I arrive breathless when your whim rings the bell...

you're like a peacock with bucharest fanned out
                                        behind you.
hotels blinking, women twinkling, the very cobblestones
graduating in cybernetics
the ministries, the institutes, the market stalls breathing the
golden powder of cinemas dissolve in air
the most yellow sunsets
                        the darkest dawns

the statistics of death rolling its curls through
foundations, the canals, underground networks,
the anaemic blue stress of the shops selling
radios, tv's, hi-fi's, cassettes, records, mikes,
earphones, plugs, sockets all mixed up together
in the saliva of nostalgia the colour of shunting
trains frozen on the *obor* station platforms and
even the beggars selling shoelaces and the
cripples selling their saucy 3-D cards and lotto
tickets denied me in favour of your tarted-up,
jaded, hostile laughter.

forget your own world,
powder your empire lest acne appear on the suntanned skin
of our friendship,
declare me independent
let me make it with my reserves of *manioc, potates*
                                        and *tapioca*
change me into something less painful,
cover me with a warmer *floreasca,*
flutter your eyelashes like electric sparks and bend
                                        your knee
so that I can finally run
my business with colourful hesitation
in those nights which they say sometimes return...

1

Seated on the wheel of a truck, the knight plays chess
with death.
over the huge olympic stadium, the sun rises like a tube
of glue, linking
existence and action, the knight plays chess with death.
then they get bored and switch to a game of badminton,
now and again
                                        they go for a dip,
have a cold drink (the vendor in a crumpled uniform, lifetimes
                                        spent opening bottles,
smiling with her pale lips, her name & photograph on an ugly
                                        badge)
then they try the high-jump, the knight using the fosbury flop
and death the straddle,
the black electronic scoreboard rotates lazily towards the
seating where a handful of spectators, mostly schoolkids and
conscripts, tell jokes about an american a russian a romanian
then they get to throwing the hammer, to bodybuilding,
underwater hockey,
bowling, shufflepuck and, towards evening, when the heat
turns lighter blue,
the knight and death sit on some cold tiled steps
and tell each other in low, confessional voices of their erotic
            adventures, dwelling on obsessions & phobias,
drinking like maniacs until they can barely crawl back
                                        to their hotels

7

I think there are many kinds of solitude, and probably the
worst kind
is the one you get in summer, in July or August
when you go to drink warm beer under the damp or dusty
awnings
                                        of the *majestic*
and on the three painted metal chairs, for the moment,
                                        nobody's sitting
when the shop windows on victoria avenue melt in bubbles of
                                        greenish glass
            over the screenless
bodywork of humble fiats, when through the transparent
                                        tarmac you can see
the roller-bearings of the giant intercontinental . . .
in the flat darkened by green drapes the wankel engine you
                        have been deliberately ignoring
as long as, studying and loving, you crouched in the soft neon
                                        womb,
this engine of objectless meditation meshes its pistons,
                                        explodes
in photos of rotten trunks & volatile mushrooms,
of branches cascading over ponds in hallucinatory pinewoods
with layer upon layer of brown needles in the silent howl of
                                        the electric chainsaws
in the violent quiet of the brain, of the planet.

9

"there comes a time when you wonder
and you think not even..."
there were stars
the car halted at night in the middle of the field,
the others got out
only the two of us stayed inside, strongly lit
I was watching you in the rear-view mirror
from behind, waving at us, a green being
descended from stars
for there were stars
a being without body
and without soul
"what's your name, green being?" we asked
"my name is daisy," she answered sadly
"just call me: daisy"

11

we were sitting face to face on an orange ice floe at the
                                                    faraway pole
encircled by a sea full of dolphins
your skirt touching my knees, light rouge on your cheekbones
tormenting your yellow eyes; a complex mechanism causing
tension between us,
a kind of frozen hopelessness
your tartan skirt hung stiffly, words just spoken panicked and
threw themselves into the quiet water,
your breasts had barely the will to fill your sweater…
your part of the iceflow, breaking away, reveals
to your paralysed sight an edge of glass, with strata of
                                                    strange fossils,
ageless, nameless; we were sitting face to face, seeing
pass, through the narrow channel, first a torpedo fish then a
                                                    sneaking seal
and soon between us were navigating tugboats and trawlers
and you on your iceberg let your hair fly loose, your nail
                                                    varnish peel,
your womb fill with brute, rough,bluish metal.

40

Window Full of Stars

Autumn, and I'm in a dark room by the window.
Not that that's important. Outside is a deep blue sky,
                                        full of stars.
The only lights on earth are the few still lit windows of the
intercontinental,
the pavilion on top of the *foisorului de foc* and,
down in *stefan cel mare*, the rows of neon,
faintly pink-violet since seven o'clock,
and the parking lights of cars.
I am alone in a difficult period of my life,
a difficult person, never easy to understand or love,
and if it's love we're talking about, I've never known love,
real or constant, except for the stars.
Since I was little I've read all sorts of books — biology,
chemistry, mechanics — I've loved radio telescopes
and speculated on all those hundreds of billions of light
                                                    years.
I've watched science programmes on television,
and the fact that ontogenia respects the filogenesis seemed
                                                        to me
more genuine than dostoevsky's 'double'.
But only now do I understand that all of these have had direct
connections with my obsession: stars.
A common, even romantic obsession, for me it has other more
                                    specific connotations.
Once, given to theories, lacking life's intuition, I was
a man who had no idea what to do with his body.
At night, wearing only pyjamas, I would go to the window
to look out at the stars.
Now I'm alone and cornered by life, and these affairs
and compromises are above my head.
On the phone to a friend, I surprise even myself by saying
life is no longer worth living.

Although I know it is pointless, I perform the most despised
job in the world: I twist my heart and brain writing —
but someday the sun
will burn to an end and, after a momentary expansion,
the substance of the universe will contract again to
                                          point zero.
I don't believe there is anything greater or lesser than,
or even equal to, humankind. To me the mystic looks
miserable, the erotic attraction between a man and a woman
                              is the only mystery.
That is why I believe that the only stable things are
                                the stars.

It is wise to believe in them alone,
it is fruitful to believe
in yellow stars twinkling so comfortingly, so tenderly,
                              so invitingly,
angelic above villages and forests,
above rivers, lakes, cities and above oceans,
and, here in our little Bucharestian universe,
glimmering above schools, the north railway station,
the institute of architecture
and above the wild crowd gathered in *lipscani*.
Now, by chance, it's Autumn, and from the window of my
                              block of flats

I too receive the golden message.